Some Fascinating Fungi Bits to Know

A Coloring Book

By Michael Reed

Some Fascinating Fungi Bits to Know

A Coloring Book

By Michael Reed

Copyright© 2017 by MR

Published in Chicago

Acknowledgement

I thank God for giving me the interest and understanding of this subject for this

book.

Fungi are not plants, but a group of special organisms that inhabited the Earth.

Many fungi species thrived on dead and/or decaying matter; thereby, helping to

return essential nutrients to their environments of Earth.

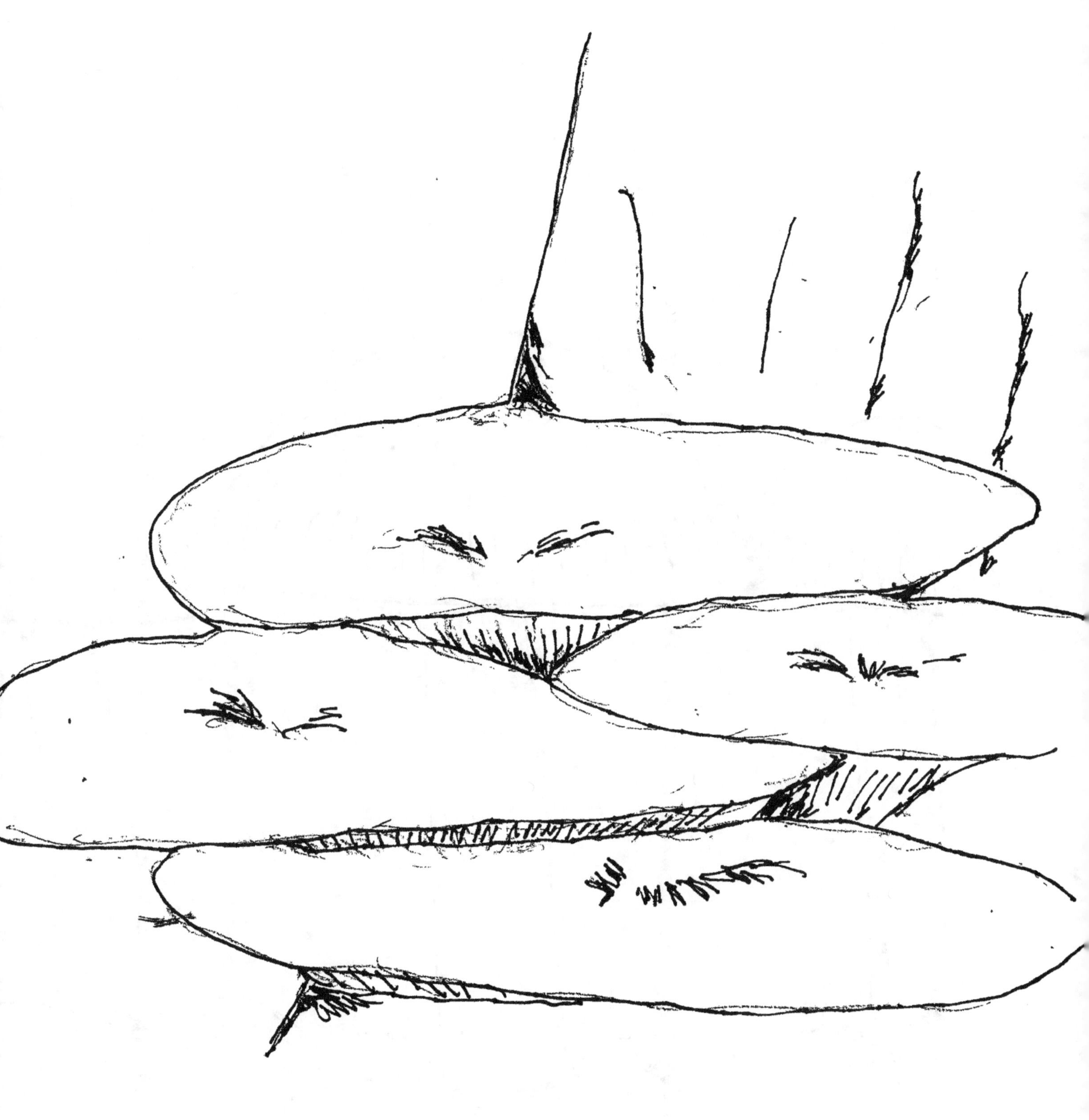

Fungi come in many forms.

Bread Mold (*Rhizopus stolonifer*)

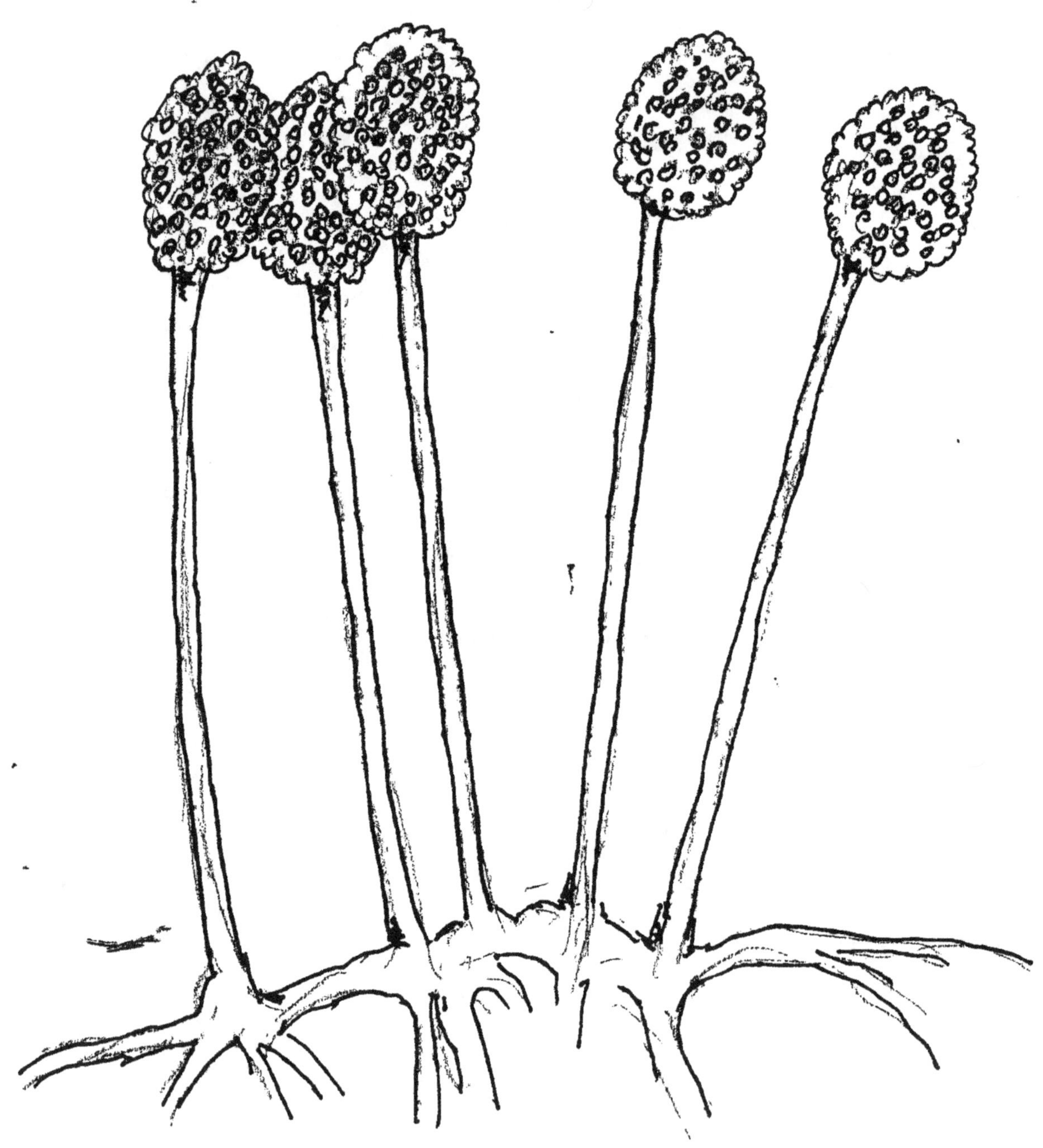

Moral Mushroom

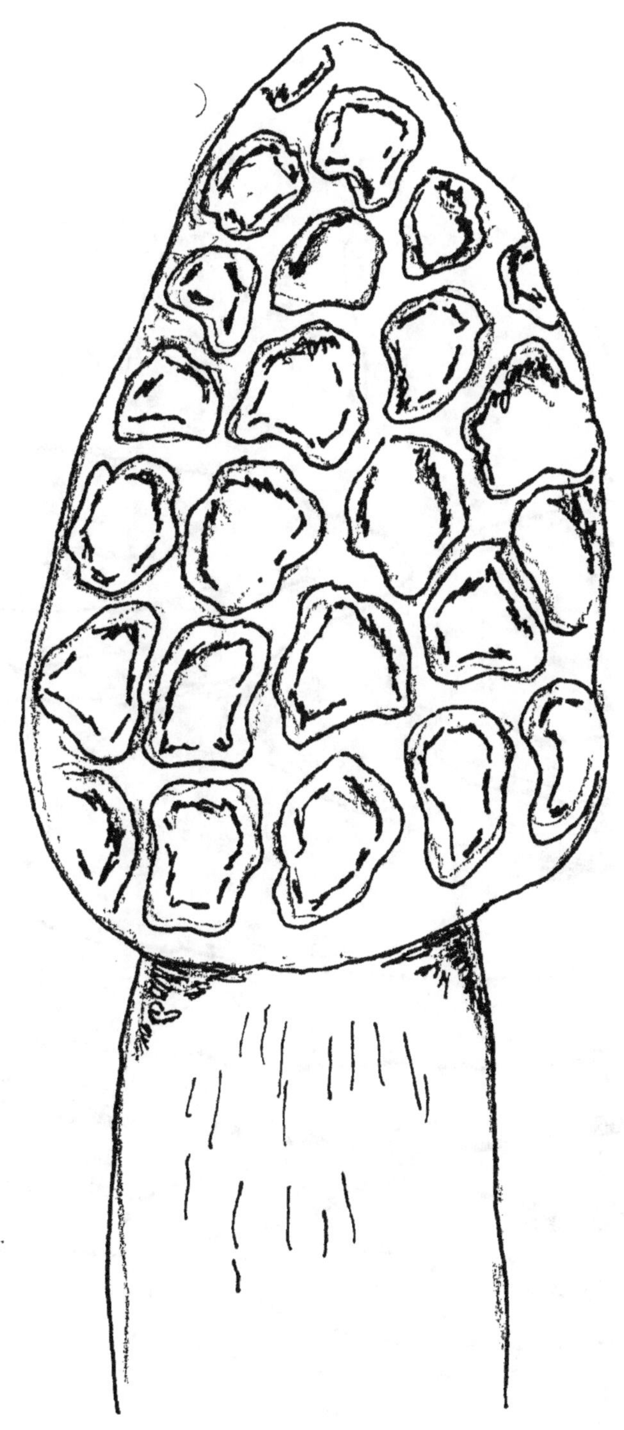

Turkey tail fungus (Tramets versicolor)

Bird Nest Fungus

Pencillium sp colony

Giant Puffball Fungus

Many fungi species reproduced through spores.

Conidiophore, reproductive bodies, of Aspergillus species

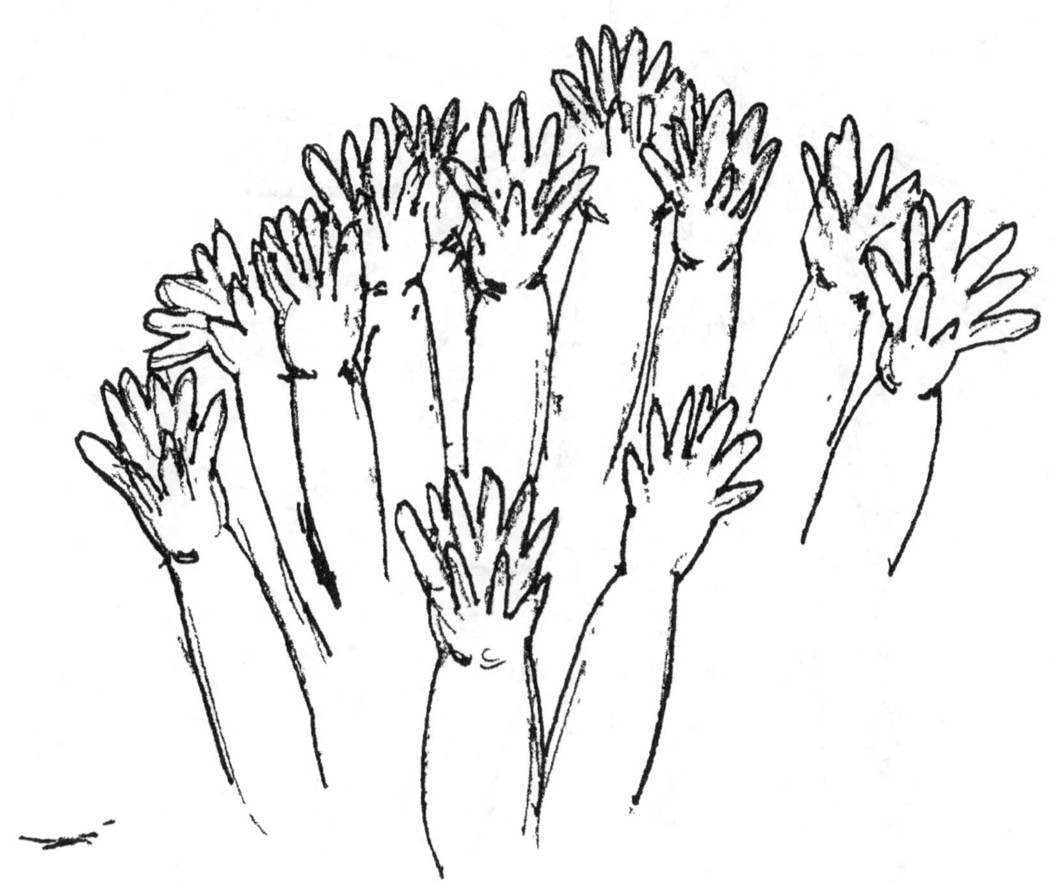

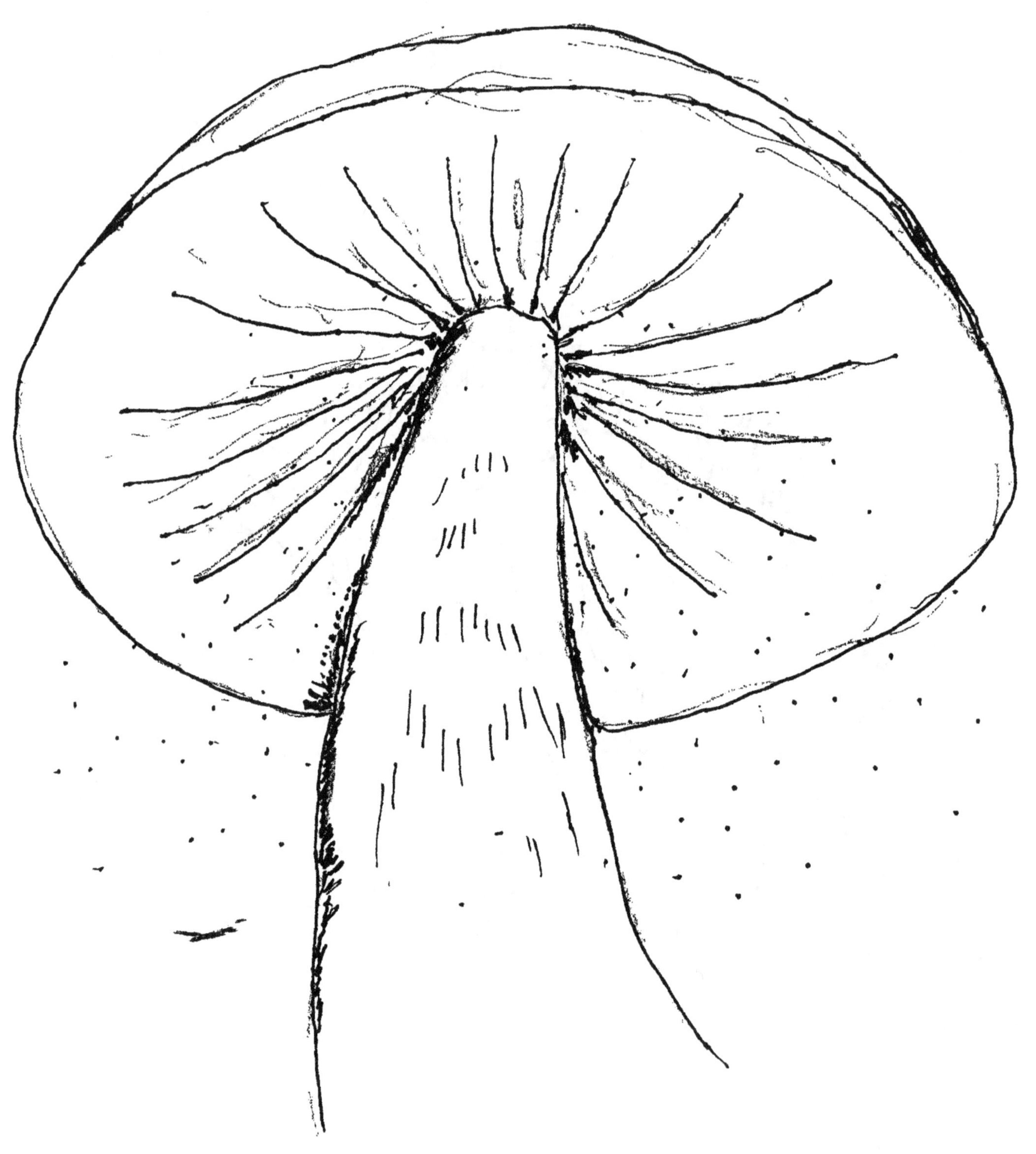

A mushroom releasing its spores.

Although there are many kinds of fungi that can do some damage to crops and

us, some species are useful in many ways. Here are some examples.

Fly Agaric (Amanita muscaria), a poisonous mushroom.

Corn Smut, a parasite on corn, but some people use it
for food.

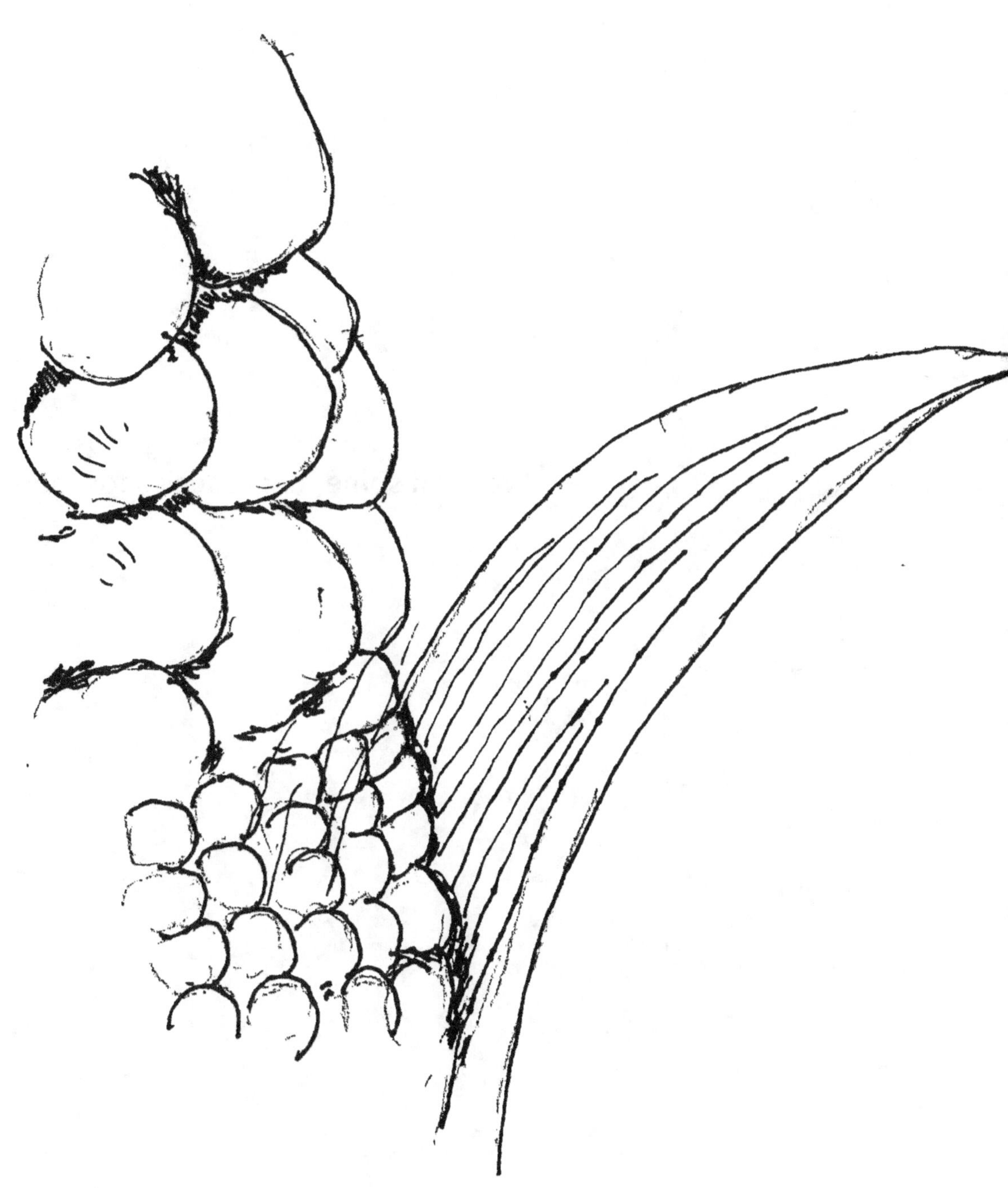

We used some fungi species for food.

Penicillum roquefort and P. camemberti are two of the Penicillum species that
are used in the production of specific cheeses.

Sliced Button Mushroom (Agaricus bisporus) are good for salads
and pizzas.

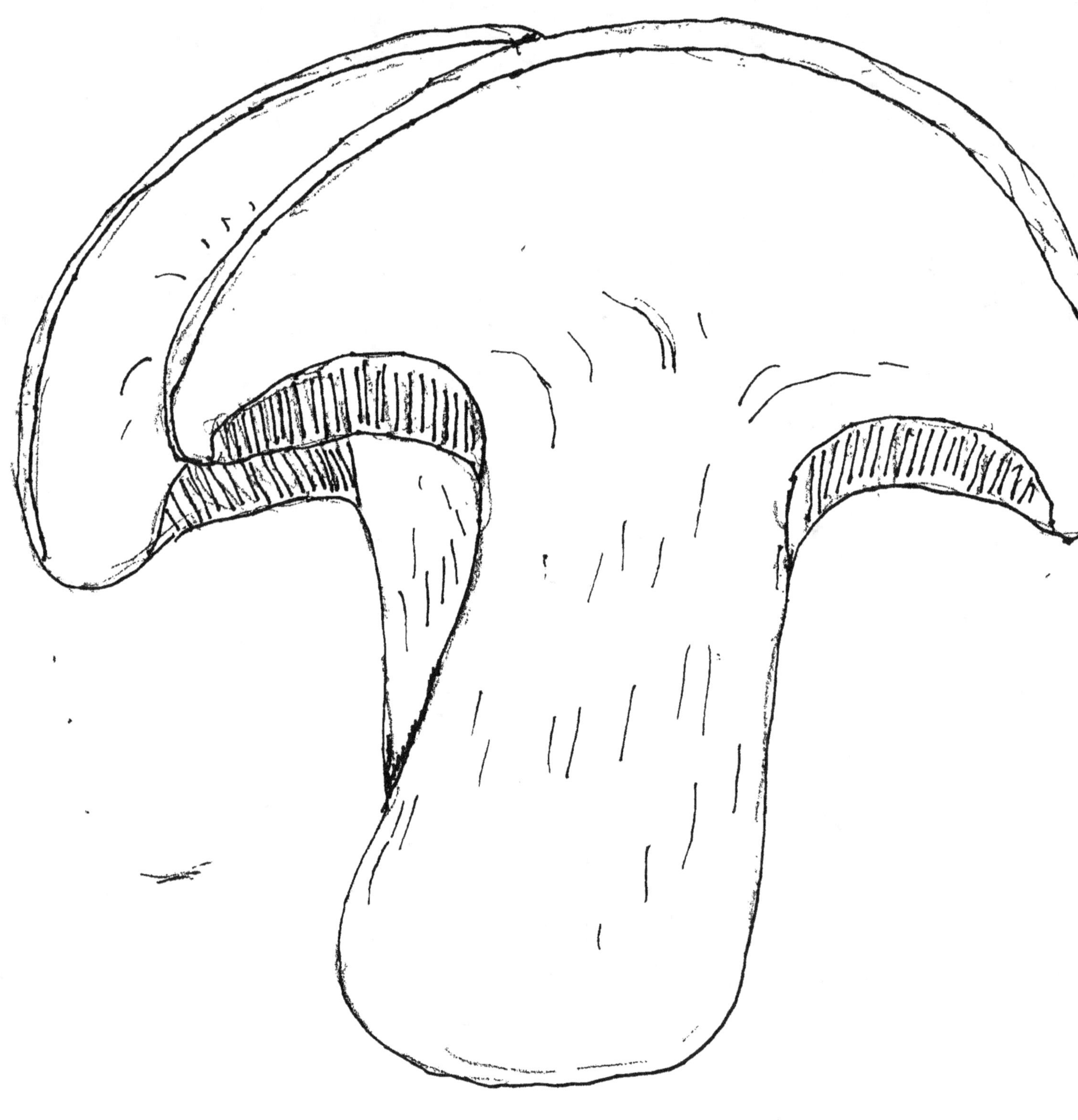

A Mushroom Burrito is a tasty dish.

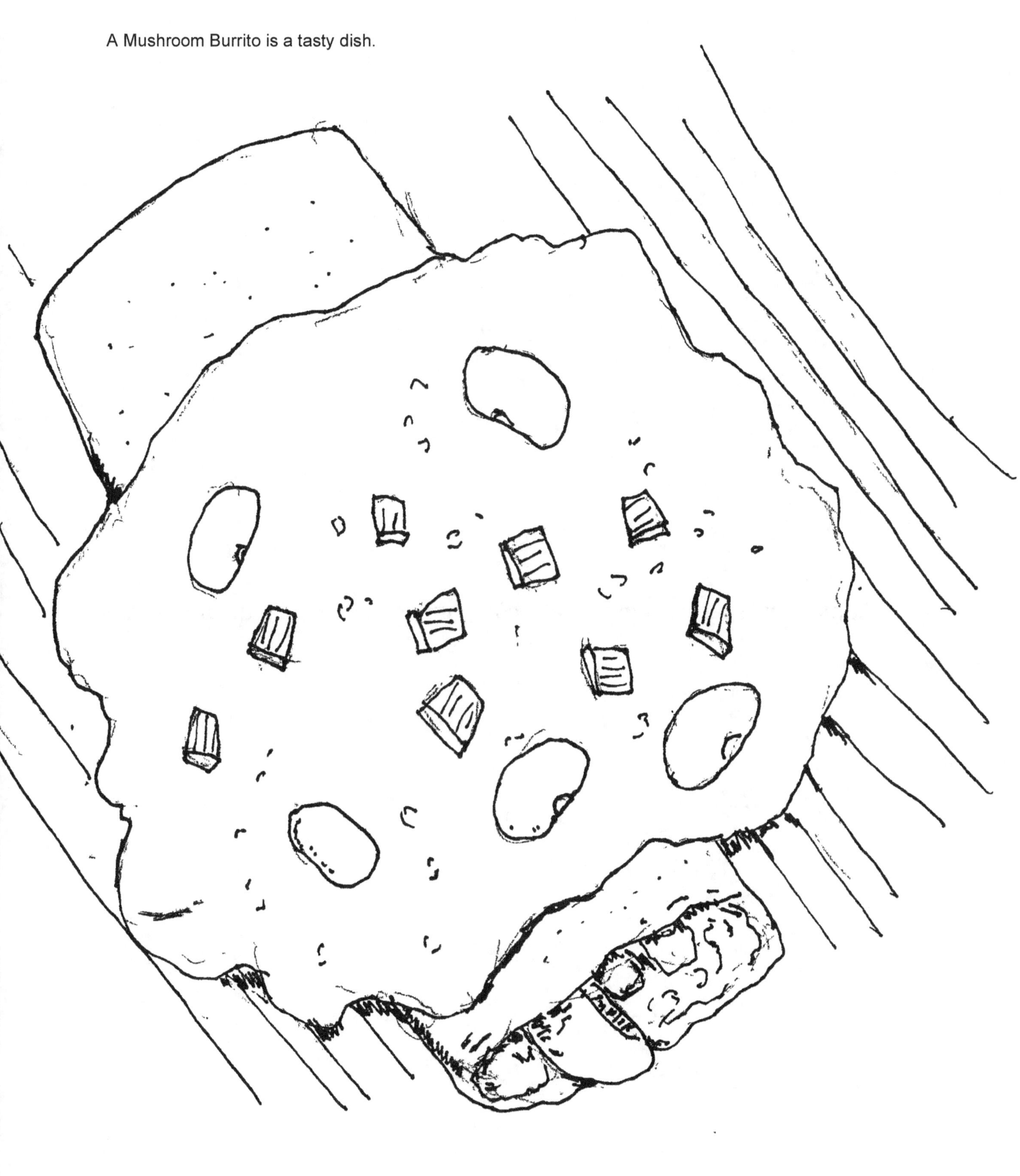

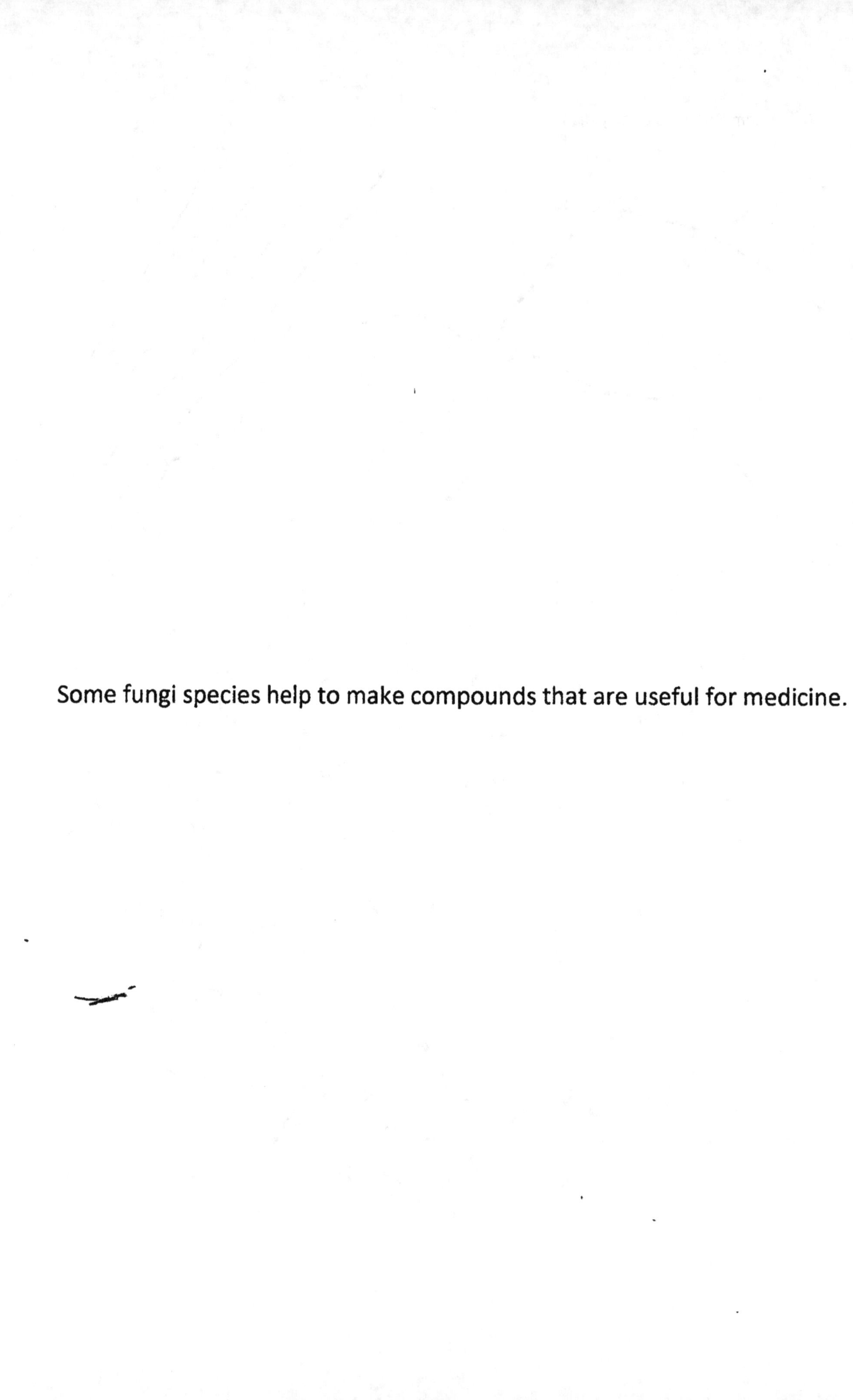

Some fungi species help to make compounds that are useful for medicine.

Shittake (Lentinula edodes) mushroom contains compounds
that can help to treat some illnesses.

P. chrysogenum is one of the Penicillium species that is used to

produce some antibiotics.

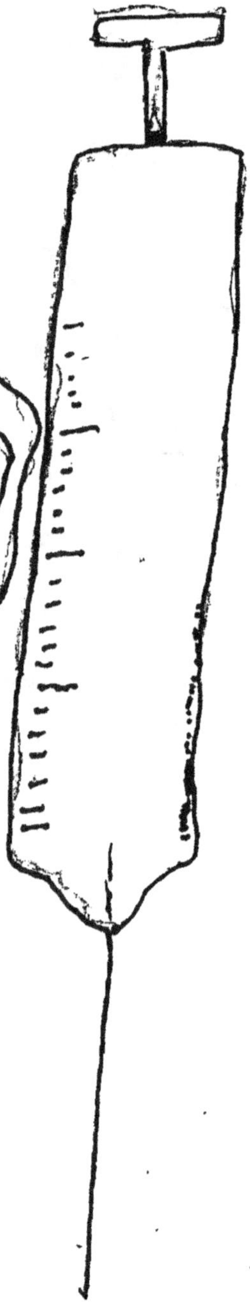

Some kinds of fungi are useful for plants' growth by helping to improve their

uptake of water and minerals.

Ectomycorrhizal fungi help some tree species by allowing the plants to receive nutrients and water. In turn, the trees help to provide nutrients to the fungi.

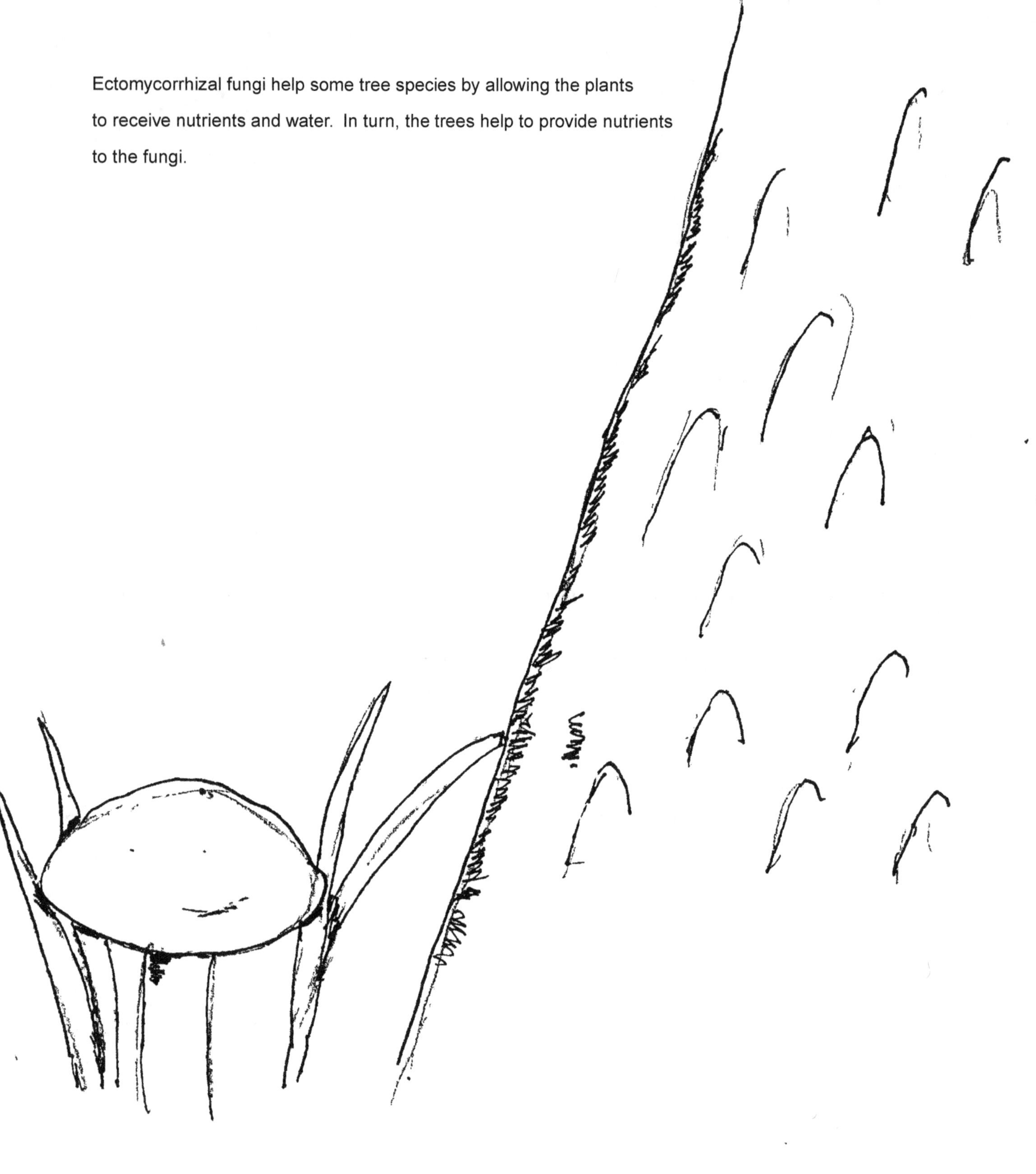

Like ectomycorrhizal, endomycorrhizal fungi provide nutrients to a plant's root but they do not form a sheath around its roots.

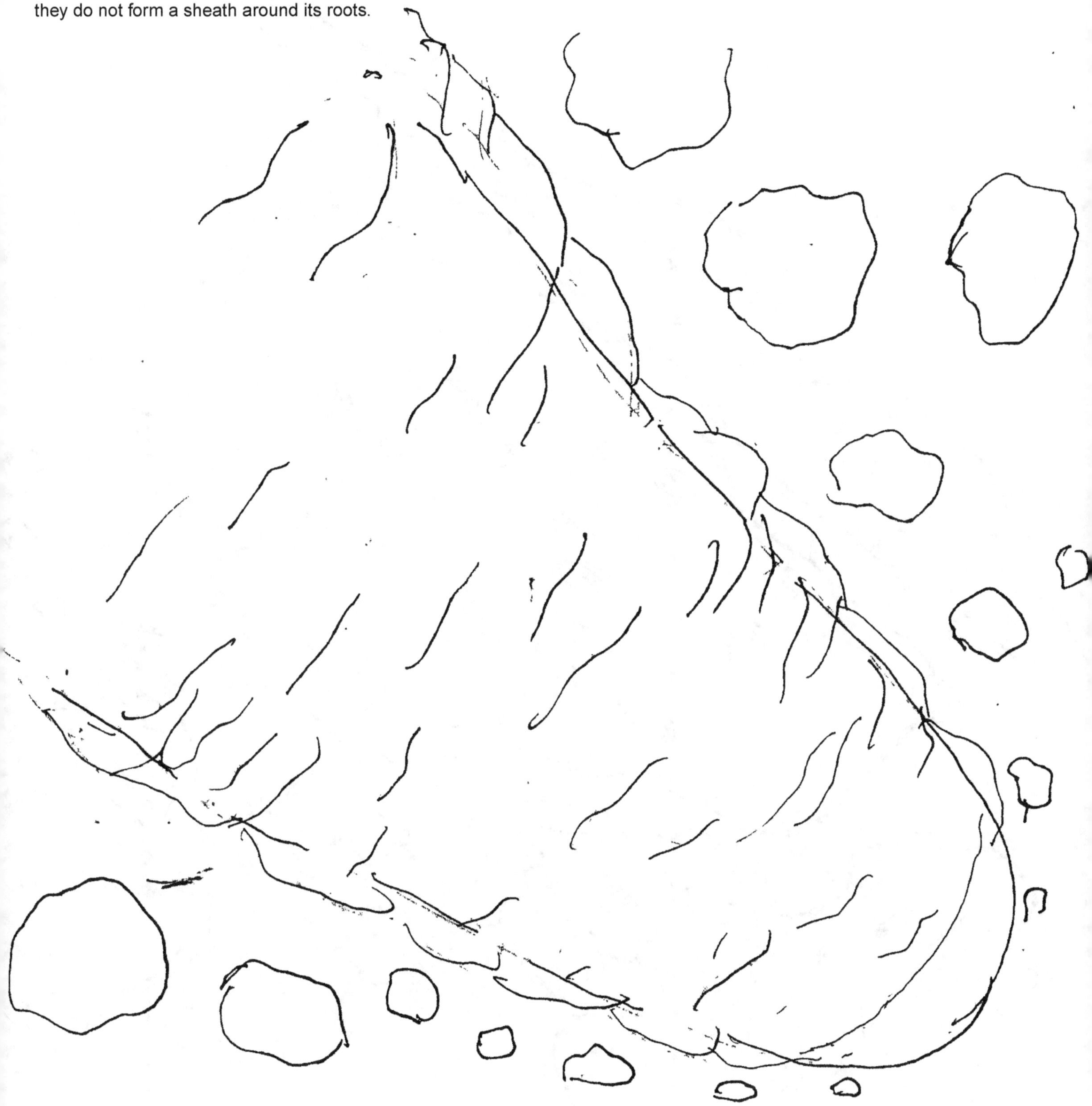

Lichen are organisms that consist of fungus and green algae/cyanobacteria as a partner.

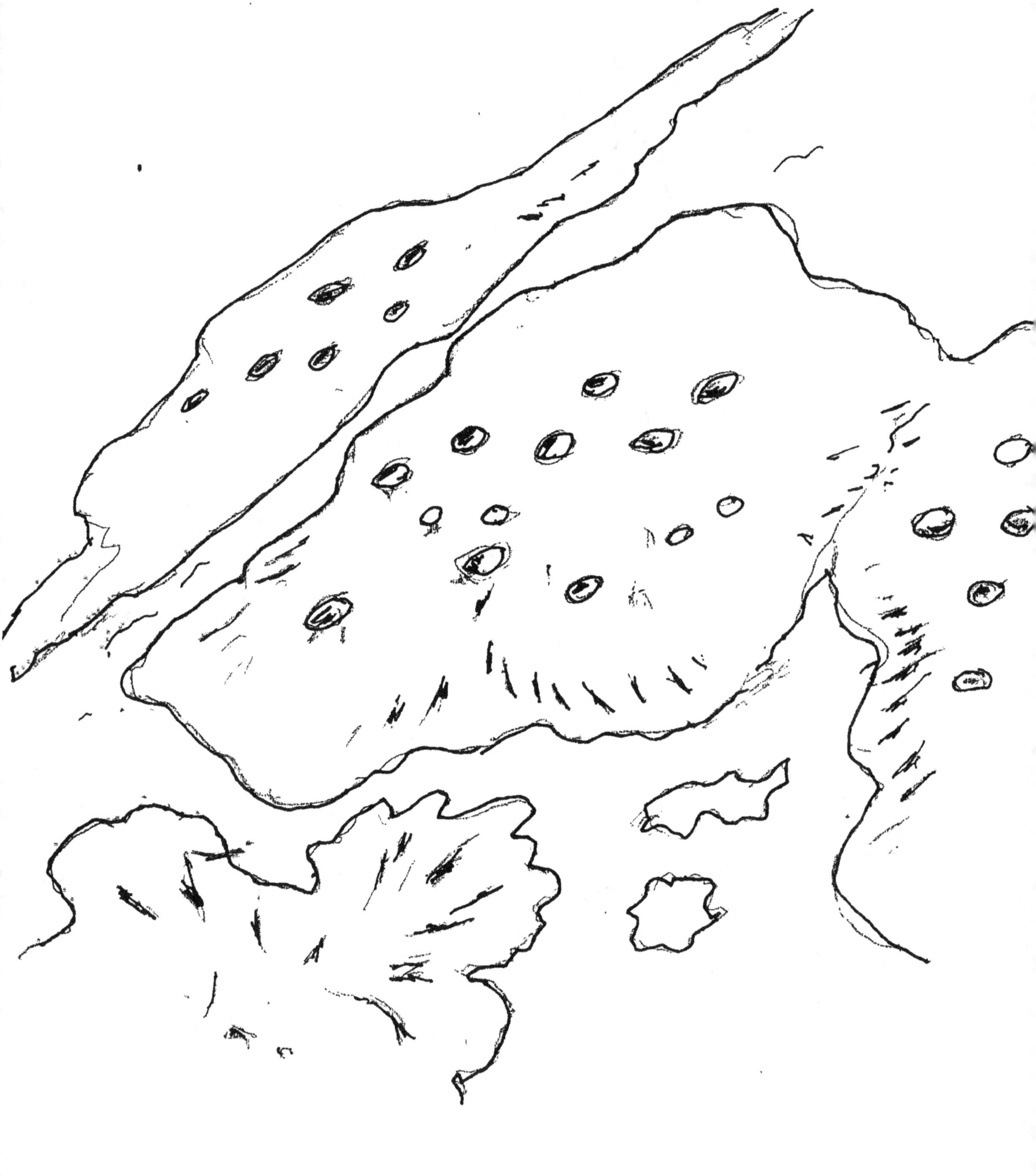

Therefore, fungi are fascinating subjects for study.

A mold community on a slice of bread

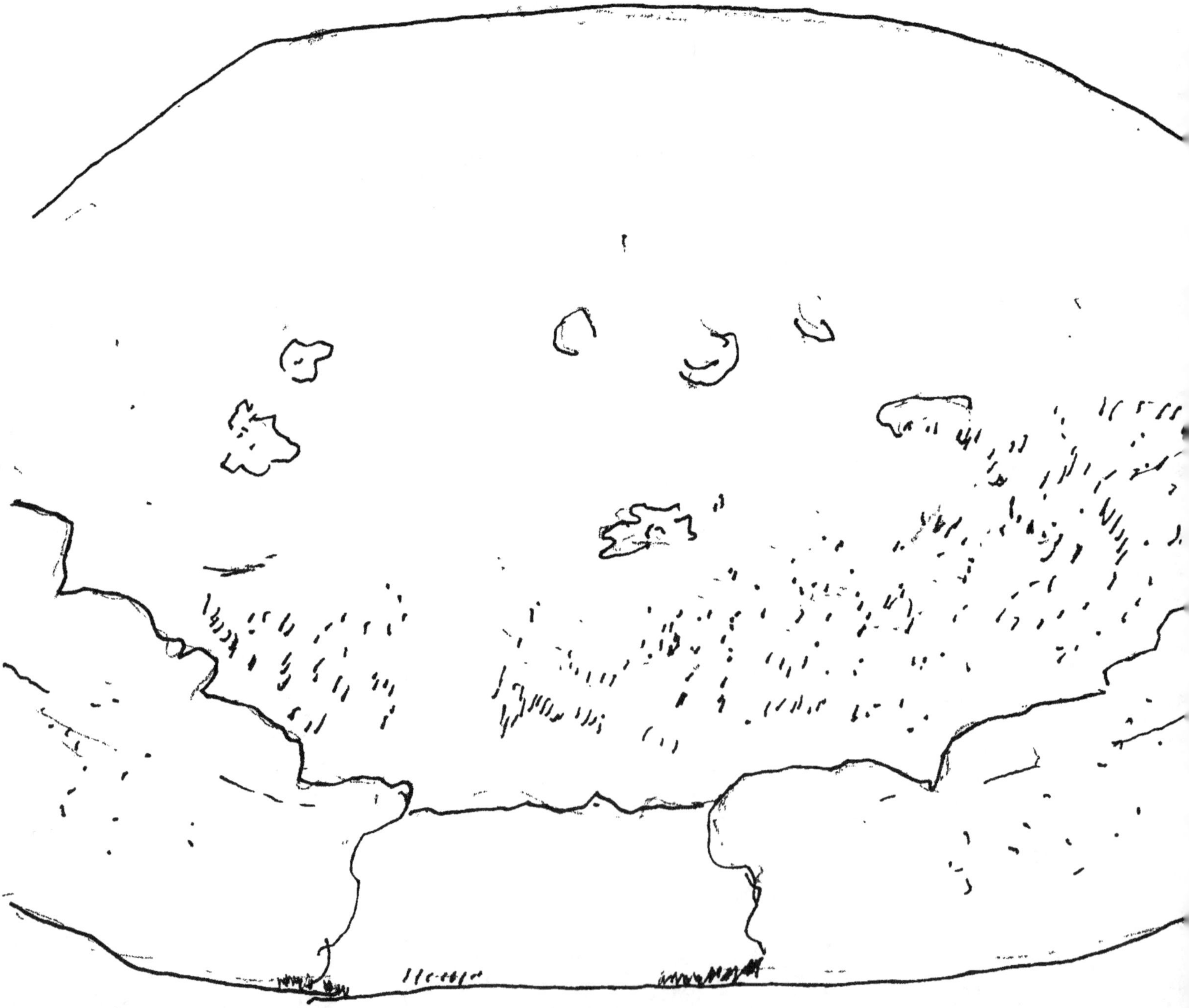

Bolete mushroom

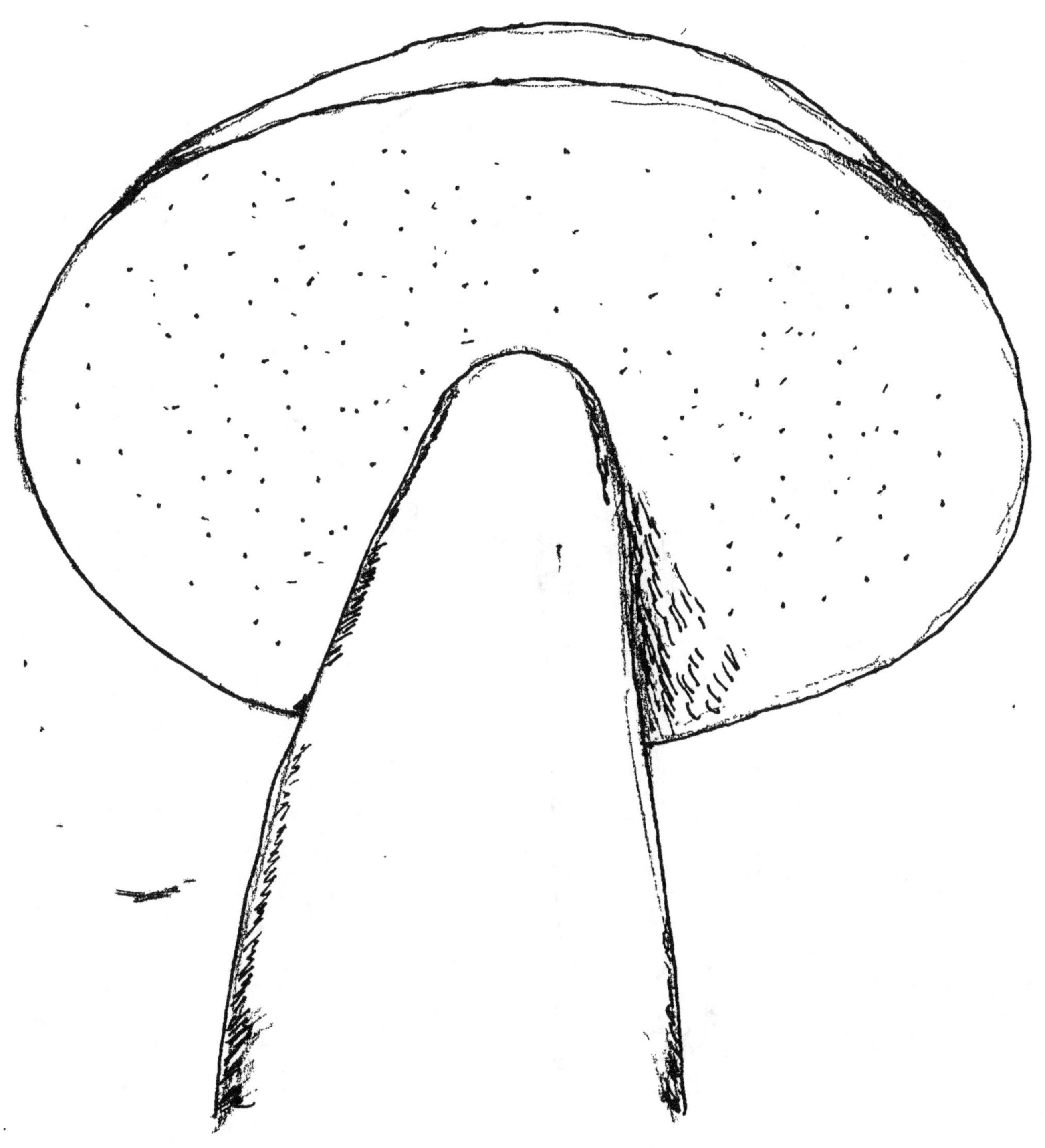

We can learn more about fungi in books, some museums, your teachers, and

computers. However, we can turn to God for understanding   about these

organisms.

FUNGUS
OF
THE
WORLD
MUSHROOM

References for Use

Katsaros, Peter. **Familiar Mushrooms: National Audubon Society Pocket Guide**.

Alfred A. Knopf, New York. 1998.

Lincoff, Gary. **The Complete Mushroom Hunter: An Illustrated Guide to Finding,

Harvesting, and Enjoying Wild Mushrooms.** Quarry Books, Beverly. 2010.

Stephenson, Steven L. **The Kingdom Fungi: The Biology of Mushrooms, Molds,

and Fungi.** Timber Press, Portland. 2010.